THE ULTIMATE 10 Sports

BASEBALL

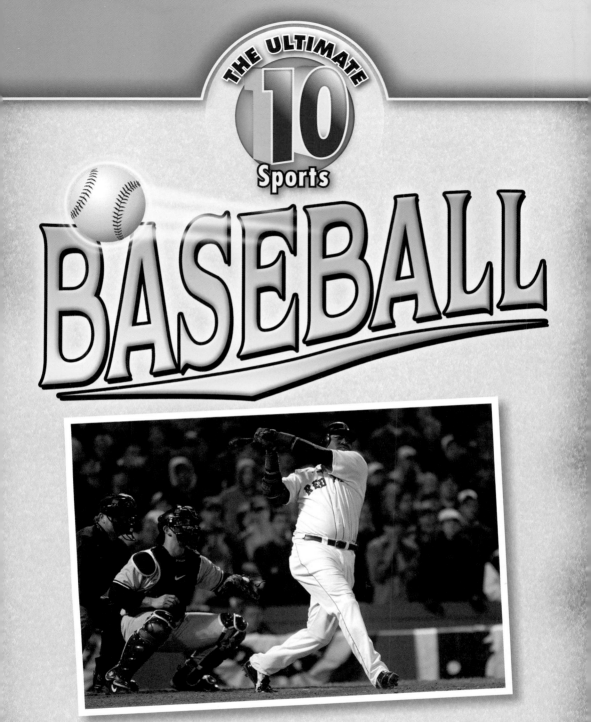

By Mark Stewart

Gareth Stevens
Publishing

Please visit our web site at www.garethstevens.com.
For a free catalog describing Gareth Stevens Publishing's list of high-quality books, call 1-800-542-2595 (USA)
or 1-800-387-3178 (Canada). Gareth Stevens Publishing's fax: 1-877-542-2596

Library of Congress Cataloging-in-Publication Data
Stewart, Mark, 1960–
   Baseball / by Mark Stewart.
        p. cm. — (The ultimate 10: sports)
   Includes bibliographical references and index.
   ISBN-10: 0-8368-9156-2 (lib. bdg.)
   ISBN-13: 978-0-8368-9156-0 (lib. bdg.)
   1. Baseball—United States—History—Juvenile literature. I. Title.
   GV867.5.S82   2008
   796.357—dc22   2008047356

This edition first published in 2009 by
Gareth Stevens Publishing
A Weekly Reader® Company
1 Reader's Digest Road
Pleasantville, NY 10570-7000 USA

Copyright © 2009 by Gareth Stevens, Inc.

Executive Managing Editor: Lisa M. Herrington
Senior Editor: Brian Fitzgerald
Creative Director: Lisa Donovan
Senior Designer: Keith Plechaty
Photo Researcher: Charlene Pinckney
Publisher: Keith Garton

Picture credits
Key: t = top, b = bottom
Cover, title page: Jim Rogash/WireImage/Getty Images; pp. 4–5: Ezra Shaw/Getty Images; p. 7: AP Images; p. 8: AP/
Zuma Press; p. 9: Bettmann/Corbis; p. 11: TSN Archives/Zuma Press; p. 12: (t) Bettmann/Corbis, (b) Bettmann/Corbis;
p. 13: TSN Archives/ Zuma Press; p. 15: Jim Rogash/WireImage/Getty Images; p. 16: (t) Icon Sports Media/Zuma Press,
(b) Shannon Stapleton/Corbis; p. 17: Getty Images; p. 19: Bettmann/Corbis; p. 20: AP Images; p. 21: TSN Archives/Zuma
Press; p. 23: Bettmann/Corbis; p. 24: Sports Imagery/Getty Images; p. 25: Bettmann/Corbis; p. 27: Bettmann/Corbis;
p. 28: (t) Bettmann/Corbis, (b) AP Images; p. 29: AP Images; p. 31: Bettmann/Corbis; p. 32: (t) Bettmann/Corbis,
(b) Mark Rucker/Getty Images; p. 33: Bettmann/Corbis; p. 35: T.G. Higgins/Getty Images; p. 36: (t) AP Images,
(b) Ronald C. Modra/Sports Imagery/Getty Images; p. 37: Focus on Sport/Getty Images; p. 39: Robert Riger/Getty
Images; p. 40: AP Images; p. 41: AP Images; p. 43: Scott Wachter/Getty Images; p. 44: (t) Doug Pensinger/Getty Images,
(b) Bettmann/Corbis; p. 45: AFP/Getty Images p. 46: (t) Rusty Kennedy/AP Images, (b) Mark Duncan/AP Images.

Printed in the United States of America

1 2 3 4 5 6 7 8 9 10 09 08

Cover: David Ortiz of the Boston Red Sox watches his game-winning home run in Game 4 of the 2004 American League
   Championship Series.

TABLE OF CONTENTS

Words in the glossary appear in **bold** type
the first time they are used in the text.

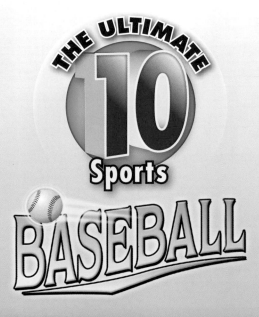

THE ULTIMATE 10 Sports BASEBALL

Welcome to The Ultimate 10! This exciting series highlights the very best from the world of sports.

Settle into your front-row seat for some of baseball's greatest games. Feel the excitement build with each pitch. See the top hitters and fielders make game-changing plays. You may never watch baseball the same way again!

Baseball is a team sport. But one player can turn a game upside down. One great play can change history. During any game, you might see something truly amazing. Years later, you will meet people who will say, "Wow, I remember that game, too!"

This book tells the stories of 10 "ultimate" baseball moments. Unforgettable players made unforgettable plays. They treated the fans to fantastic finishes. Some even changed the future of the sport.

The Boston Red Sox celebrate their win in the 2004 American League Championship Series.

Home Run!

Here are 10 baseball moments that fans will still be talking about years from now.

 Robinson Breaks the Color Barrier, 1947

 The Shot Heard 'Round the World, 1951

 The End of the Curse, 2004

 Pirates Sink the Yankees Ship, 1960

 Hammerin' Hank Passes the Babe, 1974

 The Perfect Game, 1956

 Can Anyone Stop Joltin' Joe? 1941

#8 The Buckner Ball, 1986

#9 An A-MAYS-ING Catch, 1954

 The New Iron Man, 1995

#1 Robinson Breaks the Color Barrier

Brooklyn Strikes a Blow for Equality

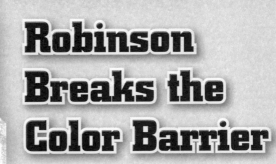

During the early 1900s, African Americans were shut out of many opportunities in the United States. In many cases, change came only after one person stood alone against racism. In baseball, Jackie Robinson broke the "color barrier" in 1947. General manager Branch Rickey signed Robinson to play for the Brooklyn Dodgers. Both men knew the game would never be the same.

FAST FACTS

OPENING DAY

DATE: April 15, 1947

LOCATION: Ebbets Field, Brooklyn, New York

TEAMS: Brooklyn Dodgers vs. Boston Braves

SCORE: Dodgers 5, Braves 3

Spider Jorgensen, Pee Wee Reese, and Eddie Stanky pose with Jackie Robinson before his first game. They made up the Dodgers infield in 1947.

The Changing Face of Baseball

For more than 50 years, African American players were kept out of major-league baseball. They played only on all-black teams in the **Negro Leagues**. Jackie Robinson changed that. In 1946, he played for Brooklyn's **farm team** in Montreal, Canada. Robinson led the league in batting. He was called up to the major-league team for the 1947 season.

Game On

As Opening Day drew near, some Dodgers did not want to play with Robinson. Branch Rickey threatened to trade or fire anyone who refused to play. Robinson was in the lineup for the team's first game, against the Boston Braves. He batted second and played first base.

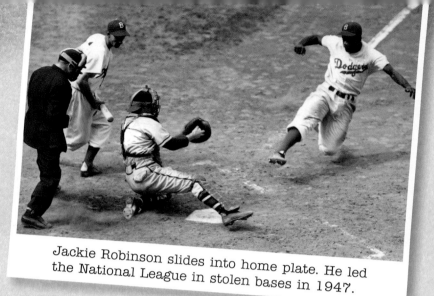

Jackie Robinson slides into home plate. He led the National League in stolen bases in 1947.

Speed Demon

Robinson could change a game with his great speed. Boston learned that in the seventh inning. Robinson batted with the Dodgers behind 3–2. He bunted the ball to help a teammate move up on the base paths. The first baseman, fearing Robinson's speed, rushed his throw. The ball hit Robinson in the back. He kept running and reached second base. Moments later, Robinson scored the winning run on a hit by Pete Reiser. No one doubted that the Dodgers **rookie** was a very special player.

FOR THE RECORD

Jackie Robinson helped make the Dodgers winners. Before he arrived, the team had reached the World Series only three times. Here is how Brooklyn did in the National League during his 10 years with the team.

SEASON	RECORD	FINISH
1947*	94–60	1st
1948	84–70	3rd
1949**	97–57	1st
1950	89–65	2nd
1951	97–60	2nd
1952	96–57	1st
1953	105–49	1st
1954	92–62	2nd
1955	98–55	1st Won World Series
1956	93–61	1st

*Won Rookie of the Year award   **Won Most Valuable Player award

Fantastic Finish

Robinson's first summer as a major leaguer was not an easy one. He received death threats. When the Dodgers played road games, some fans and players aimed racial insults at him. Still, Robinson promised Rickey he would not fight back. Instead, Robinson let his skill do the talking. He was named the Rookie of the Year and led the Dodgers to the **pennant**. More important, he proved that black players belonged in the major leagues.

Jackie Robinson crosses home plate after his first major-league home run. He scored 125 runs in 1947.

DID YOU KNOW?

In 1997, every team in baseball "retired" Robinson's uniform number, 42. No one in baseball would wear that number again. Players who already wore number 42 were allowed to keep wearing it. The last to do so was Mariano Rivera of the New York Yankees.

#2 The Shot Heard 'Round the World

Bobby Thomson Beats the Dodgers

The race for the National League pennant in 1951 was one of the most exciting in history. The Giants and the Dodgers were bitter rivals. Every game they played was like a war. Baseball fans expected a close finish. But no one realized it would come down to one unforgettable swing of the bat.

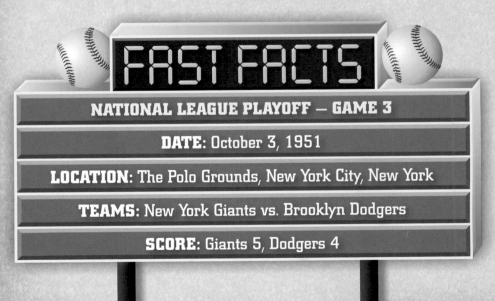

FAST FACTS

NATIONAL LEAGUE PLAYOFF — GAME 3

DATE: October 3, 1951

LOCATION: The Polo Grounds, New York City, New York

TEAMS: New York Giants vs. Brooklyn Dodgers

SCORE: Giants 5, Dodgers 4

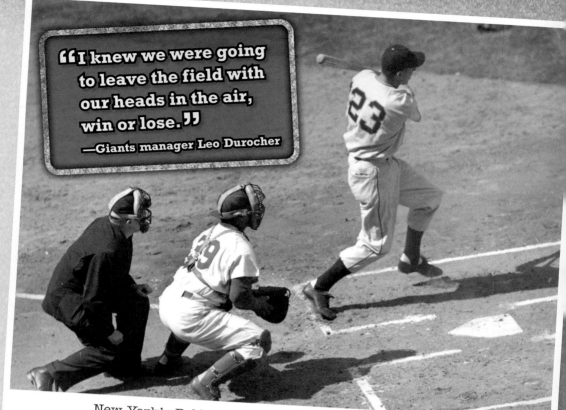

> **"I knew we were going to leave the field with our heads in the air, win or lose."**
> —Giants manager Leo Durocher

New York's Bobby Thomson bats against the Dodgers. He hit 32 home runs in 1951—the most in his career.

The Amazing Race

In early August, many Giants fans were ready to give up. Their team was 13½ games behind the hated Dodgers. Only seven weeks remained in the season. Suddenly, it seemed as if the Giants couldn't lose. At one point, they won 16 straight games. At the end of the season, the teams were tied for first place. A three-game playoff would decide which team would go to the World Series.

Game On

The Giants and the Dodgers each won a playoff game. The third and final game was played on a dreary day in front of 34,320 fans. The Dodgers scored in the first inning on a hit by Jackie Robinson. New York's Bobby Thomson drove in a run in the seventh inning to tie the score.

FOR THE RECORD

Until 1951, Bobby Thomson had been the Giants center fielder. That season, he moved to third base to make room for rookie Willie Mays. The 20-year-old star was on deck when Thomson hit his famous home run. Mays would go on to become a **Hall of Famer**. But on that day, he was terrified of making the last out of the game. He has said many times that he was the happiest person in the ballpark!

Willie Mays picks out a bat from the bat rack. He was named Rookie of the Year in 1951.

Don Newcombe goes into his windup. He was one of the first African American pitchers in the majors.

Brooklyn Battles Back

The game wasn't tied for long. Brooklyn scored three runs in the top of the eighth inning. Pitcher Don Newcombe shut down the Giants in the bottom of the eighth. He started the ninth inning with a 4–1 lead, but he could not finish off New York. Two singles and a double made the score 4–2. The Giants had runners on second and third base with one out. Thomson came to bat with the season on the line.

> **"The Giants win the pennant! The Giants win the pennant! The Giants win the pennant!"**
>
> —Giants announcer Russ Hodges, after Bobby Thomson's home run

Fantastic Finish

The Dodgers brought in Ralph Branca to face Thomson. Branca's plan was to get a strike on Thomson and then tempt him to swing at a bad pitch.

The Brooklyn pitcher fired one right down the middle for strike one. Branca's next pitch was high and inside—but not far enough. Thomson whipped his bat around and hit a sinking line drive to left field. The ball barely cleared the wall for a three-run homer. The Giants had won 5–4. Thomson's blast will be known forever as "the Shot Heard 'Round the World."

Happy teammates greet Thomson as he touches home plate. His home run made the Giants National League champions.

DID YOU KNOW?

Thomson loved to hit against the Dodgers. He hit eight homers against them in 1951. His seventh had come in Game 1 of the playoffs, also against Ralph Branca. Thomson and Branca later became great friends.

#3 The End of the Curse

The Red Sox Finally Beat the Yankees

In 1918, the Boston Red Sox were on top of the baseball world. In 1920, they sold Babe Ruth to the New York Yankees. That decision—and the Yankees—had been haunting them ever since. Boston fans were convinced that their team was "cursed." The two teams met in the 2004 American League Championship Series (ALCS). After three straight losses, it looked as if Boston's years of suffering would continue.

FAST FACTS

AMERICAN LEAGUE CHAMPIONSHIP SERIES — GAME 7

DATE: October 20, 2004

LOCATION: Yankee Stadium, Bronx, New York

TEAMS: Boston Red Sox vs. New York Yankees

SCORE: Red Sox 10, Yankees 3

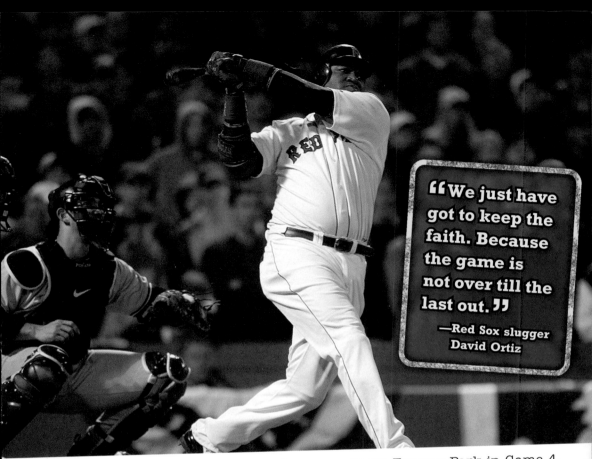

David Oritz watches his winning home run leave Fenway Park in Game 4.

Three Down, One to Go

The Yankees won the first two games of the series in New York. In Game 3, they pounded Boston 19–8. The odds were against the Red Sox. No baseball team had ever won a playoff series after losing the first three games. The Red Sox, however, would not go down without a fight.

Game On

In Game 4, the Red Sox trailed 4–3 as they batted in the bottom of the ninth inning. New York's best pitcher, Mariano Rivera, was on the mound. He had never failed with a pennant on the line. The Yankees were three outs away from the World Series. But the Red Sox scratched out a walk, a steal, and a single to tie the game 4–4. They then won it on a two-run home run by David Ortiz in the 12th inning.

Curt Schilling pitches through the pain in Game 6. He led the majors with 21 wins in 2004.

Pulling Even

Ortiz was the hero again in Game 5. His single in the 14th inning scored the winning run. In Game 6, Boston turned to star pitcher Curt Schilling. He had an injured ankle that was bleeding during the game. But he pitched through the pain, and the Red Sox won 4–2. They were just nine innings away from baseball history.

FOR THE RECORD

In 2004, Boston fans were still hurting from the team's collapse the year before. In Game 7 of the ALCS, Boston led New York 5–2 in the eighth inning. The Yankees fought back to tie the score. The game went into extra innings. Aaron Boone of the Yankees led off the 11th inning with a game-winning home run. Boston would have to live with its curse for another season.

Aaron Boone celebrates his pennant-winning home run in 2003.

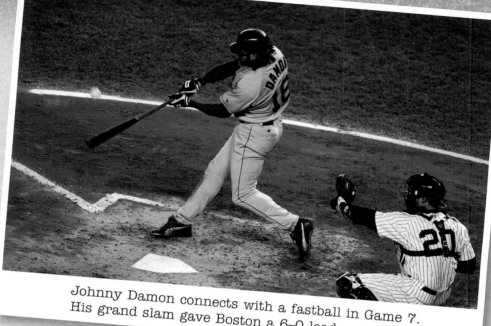

Johnny Damon connects with a fastball in Game 7.
His grand slam gave Boston a 6–0 lead.

Fantastic Finish

Game 7 was played in Yankee Stadium. The Red Sox came out swinging. In the first inning, Ortiz hit a home run to give the Red Sox a 2–0 lead. In the second inning, Johnny Damon came to bat with the bases loaded. He had struggled all series long. But he launched the first pitch into the right-field stands for a **grand slam**. The sellout crowd fell silent. The Red Sox led 6–0. They went on to win the game 10–3. No team in history had ever made a bigger comeback.

ff Not many people get the opportunity to shock the world. We came out and did it. JJ

—Red Sox first baseman Kevin Millar

DID YOU KNOW?

The Red Sox met the St. Louis Cardinals in the 2004 World Series. They swept the Cardinals in four games. Boston had its first championship in 86 years. The curse was history!

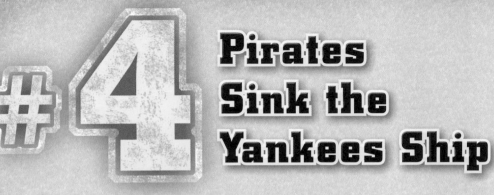

#4 Pirates Sink the Yankees Ship

A Home Run for the Ages

Few fans outside of Pittsburgh gave the Pirates a chance in the 1960 World Series. After all, the New York Yankees were a team of superstars. The Bronx Bombers had led the majors in home runs. All the Pirates could do was play hard and keep their fingers crossed. No one guessed that a skinny infielder would beat the Yankees at their own game.

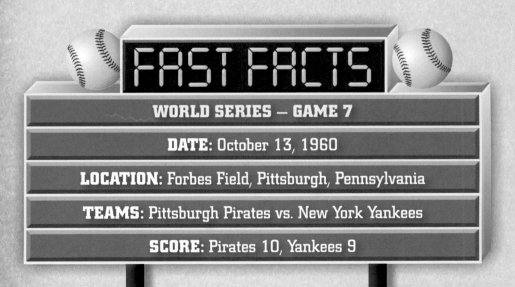

FAST FACTS

WORLD SERIES — GAME 7

DATE: October 13, 1960

LOCATION: Forbes Field, Pittsburgh, Pennsylvania

TEAMS: Pittsburgh Pirates vs. New York Yankees

SCORE: Pirates 10, Yankees 9

Loyal fans show their support for the Pirates in the 1960 World Series. Most baseball fans did not think the Series would be close.

Big Bats

The Yankees were the best team in baseball. They were led by sluggers Mickey Mantle and Roger Maris. New York showed off its power in its three Series wins. The Bronx Bombers beat the Pirates 16–3, 10–0, and 12–0. But Pittsburgh surprised everyone by winning three tight games. The Series came down to Game 7.

Game On

Game 7 was one of the wildest in World Series history. The Pirates scored four runs in the first two innings. Vern Law and Elroy Face, their two best pitchers, could not protect the lead. Yogi Berra put the Yankees ahead 5–4 with a home run in the sixth inning. New York added two more runs in the eighth inning to make the score 7–4.

> **"I'm not sure if we belonged on the same field with those fellas."**
> —Pirates outfielder Bill Virdon

FOR THE RECORD

Luckily for the Pirates, baseball is played on a field, not on paper.
Here is a look at the numbers from the 1960 World Series.
It's hard to believe that Pittsburgh won!

	HITS	RUNS	HOME RUNS	AVERAGE	WINS
YANKEES	91	55	10	.338	3
PIRATES	60	27	4	.256	4

A Seesaw Battle

In the bottom of the eighth inning, Pittsburgh had a man on base. Bill Virdon hit an easy grounder to Tony Kubek at shortstop. The Yankees got into position for a **double play**. Suddenly, the ball took a bad hop and hit Kubek in the throat. Both runners were safe. The Pirates went on to score five times. The big hit was a three-run home run by Hal Smith. However, the Yankees refused to lose. They tied the game 9–9 in the top of the ninth inning.

Tony Kubek clutches his throat after being hit by a ground ball. That bad hop for the Yankees was a lucky break for the Pirates.

Fantastic Finish

Bill Mazeroski led off the bottom of the ninth inning for Pittsburgh. Yankees pitcher Ralph Terry threw him a high fastball. Catcher John Blanchard reminded Terry to keep the ball low. The next pitch was lower, but not low enough. Mazeroski hit a line drive to deep left field. The ball cleared the fence for a Series-winning home run! Hundreds of fans poured onto the field. Mazeroski galloped around the bases and disappeared into the crowd at home plate. The Pirates were world champions.

The Pirates—and some fans—wait to celebrate with Bill Mazeroski after his famous home run.

DID YOU KNOW?

Bill Mazeroski was more famous for his glove than for his bat. "Maz" won the **Gold Glove** award eight times. In 2001, he was voted into the Baseball Hall of Fame.

"I didn't think I hit it hard enough to clear the wall."

—Bill Mazeroski

#5 Hammerin' Hank Passes the Babe

Hank Aaron Becomes Baseball's Home-Run King

Babe Ruth was the most famous hitter of all time. His record of 714 home runs seemed unbreakable. By 1973, it was clear that Hank Aaron had a chance to catch Ruth. As Aaron approached number 714, each day became a struggle. Many people did not want an African American home-run king. They let Aaron know it.

FAST FACTS

ATLANTA BRAVES HOME OPENER	
DATE: April 8, 1974	
LOCATION: Atlanta-Fulton County Stadium, Atlanta, Georgia	
TEAMS: Atlanta Braves vs. Los Angeles Dodgers	
SCORE: Braves 7, Dodgers 4	

Hank Aaron launches home run number 714 against the Cincinnati Reds. He tied Babe Ruth's record on his first swing of the season.

Death Threats

During the 1973 season, Aaron crept closer to Ruth's record. He finished the year with 713 home runs—just one behind Ruth. That winter, Aaron received nasty letters. Some fans did not want an African American to beat the beloved Babe. Some of those letters warned that Aaron would be killed before he got a chance.

Game On

As the 1974 season began, Aaron was feeling terrible pressure. He wanted to break the record as quickly as possible. Number 714 came on Aaron's first swing of the season, on the road against the Cincinnati Reds. The Braves returned to Atlanta for their first home game on April 8. They faced the Los Angeles Dodgers.

Hank Aaron watches his record-smashing home run soar toward the left-field fence.

Hank Hammers It

Aaron walked in his first at bat. He stepped to the plate again in the fourth inning. Dodgers pitcher Al Downing waited for his catcher to give him the sign. Downing kicked his leg high and threw a fastball. The pitch was right where Aaron wanted it. He blasted a high fly ball to left field. Dodgers left fielder Bill Buckner tried to climb the fence to catch it. But Aaron's long drive kept going.

FOR THE RECORD

Hank Aaron was more than just a slugger. He hit well with runners on base and was a good base runner. Here is how Aaron compares with the other all-time home-run leaders.

	HITS	RUNS	HOME RUNS	RBI*	AVG**
BARRY BONDS	2,935	2,227	762	1,996	.298
HANK AARON	3,771	2,174	755	2,297	.305
BABE RUTH	2,873	2,174	714	2,213	.342
WILLIE MAYS	3,283	2,062	660	1,903	.302

*Runs Batted In   **Batting Average

Fantastic Finish

Aaron's long ball landed in the back of Atlanta's **bullpen**. His teammate Tom House caught the historic home run. House ran it back to home plate, where the Braves were waiting for Aaron. As Aaron rounded third base, he broke into a wide smile. Baseball's new home-run king was just happy the chase was over. Aaron's mother was there to give him a big hug. After everything he had been through, that was the best prize of all.

Hank Aaron shows his home-run ball to the fans in Atlanta. He was happy to break the record so quickly.

DID YOU KNOW?

Hank Aaron finished his career two years later with 755 home runs. He held the home-run record until 2007, when Barry Bonds passed him. However, many fans still consider "Hammerin' Hank" to be the real champion.

#6 The Perfect Game

Don Larsen Is Dandy Against the Dodgers

The pressure of a World Series can do strange things. It can make a great player seem ordinary. It can also make an ordinary player great. The New York Yankees split the first four games of the 1956 World Series with the Brooklyn Dodgers. In Game 5, the Yankees turned to their least-perfect pitcher. Little did they realize he was the perfect man for the job.

FAST FACTS

WORLD SERIES – GAME 5

DATE: October 8, 1956

LOCATION: Yankee Stadium, Bronx, New York

TEAMS: New York Yankees vs. Brooklyn Dodgers

SCORE: Yankees 2, Dodgers 0

Don Larsen throws the final pitch of Game 5 of the 1956 World Series. Before the season, the Yankees almost cut Larsen from the team!

Battle of the Stars

The Yankees and the Dodgers were familiar foes by the fall of 1956. The teams had met in three of the last four World Series. The Yankees were a team of superstars, including Mickey Mantle, Whitey Ford, and Yogi Berra. The Dodgers also had great players, including Duke Snider, Jackie Robinson, and Roy Campanella. After four games, the series was tied two games to two.

Game On

For Game 5, Yankees manager Casey Stengel called on pitcher Don Larsen. Larsen was hardly a superstar. He had once lost 21 games in a season. In Game 2, he had blown a 6–0 lead. The players called the awkward Larsen "Gooney Bird." But early in Game 5, no one on the field looked better.

Mickey Mantle races to catch a fly ball by Gil Hodges. Mantle was one of the fastest center fielders in baseball.

Love That Glove

Larsen was simply brilliant. He was throwing all of his pitches for strikes. Mantle hit a home run to give the Yankees a slim lead. He also made two great fielding plays. He caught a low line drive in the third inning. In the fifth, Mantle caught a long drive by Gil Hodges. After eight innings, Larsen had not allowed a batter to reach first base. He was three outs away from a **perfect game**.

FOR THE RECORD

How rare is a perfect game? Before 1956, there had been only five in the history of baseball—and only three since 1904. No pitcher before or since Larsen has thrown one in a World Series game. Not until 1998 did another Yankee, David Wells, pitch a perfect game. Wells and Larsen had attended the same high school in San Diego, California!

Yankees players carry David Wells off the field after his perfect game.

Fantastic Finish

The first hitter in the ninth inning was Carl Furillo. He hit an easy fly ball to right field for the first out. Campanella came up and grounded out to the second baseman. With one out to go, Brooklyn sent up **pinch hitter** Dale Mitchell.

Larsen threw a ball outside. He then whipped a strike right down the middle. Mitchell swung at strike two and then fouled off a pitch. Larsen's next pitch sailed over the outside corner of the plate. The umpire called *Strike three!* Berra, the Yankees catcher, ran and jumped into Larsen's arms. Larsen had thrown the first no-hitter *and* first perfect game in the World Series.

Yogi Berra (#8) leaps into Don Larsen's arms after the final out.

❝Look at the scoreboard, Mick. Wouldn't it be something?❞

—Don Larsen, to Mickey Mantle after the seventh inning

DID YOU KNOW?

The Yankees went on to win the World Series in seven games. Berra hit a grand slam to help the Yankees win the final game 9–0. Larsen pitched in the majors until 1967, but he never became a star. However, for a few hours in 1956, he was the best pitcher anyone ever saw.

#7 Can Anyone Stop Joltin' Joe?

Joe DiMaggio Hits in 56 Straight Games

Records are made to be broken. Yet one baseball record may last forever. In 1941, Joe DiMaggio of the New York Yankees began baseball's greatest hitting streak. He used his keen eye and powerful swing to kept the streak going. The star center fielder got at least one hit in game after game after game. It seemed as if the streak might never end.

FAST FACTS

RECORD 56-GAME HITTING STREAK

PLAYER: Joe DiMaggio

TEAM: New York Yankees

DATES: May 15–July 16, 1941

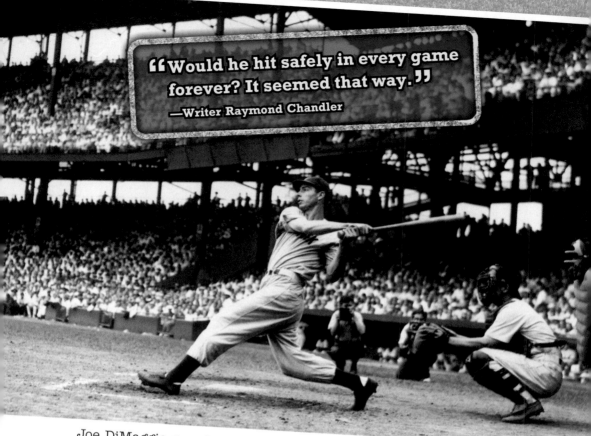

Joe DiMaggio smacks a line drive during a game in June 1941. He got at least one hit in every game that month.

No Ordinary Joe

Joe DiMaggio was 26 years old in the summer of 1941. Most fans agreed that he was the best player in baseball. He had led the league in batting twice and was named Most Valuable Player (MVP) in 1939. He was one of the fastest runners and smoothest fielders in the game. After DiMaggio joined the Yankees in 1936, they won four World Series in a row.

Game On

On May 15, 1941, DiMaggio hit a single against the Chicago White Sox. As spring turned to summer, he got at least one hit in every game. Soon his streak became the biggest story in the country. Millions of Americans asked the same question every day: "How did Joe do?"

The Streak Continues

On July 2, DiMaggio hit in his 45th game in a row. This broke the record of 44, set by Willie Keeler in 1897. How long could "Joltin' Joe" keep going? No one knew. On July 16, he collected three hits against the Cleveland Indians. The streak stood at 56 games. The next night, more than 67,000 fans jammed into Cleveland's stadium. At the time, it was the largest crowd ever to see a night baseball game. They wanted to see if the Indians could stop DiMaggio.

Joe DiMaggio scores a run on July 16. Moments earlier, he had gotten a hit in the 56th game in a row.

FOR THE RECORD

Ted Williams of the Red Sox batted an amazing .406 in 1941. Still, sportswriters thought DiMaggio's streak was a greater feat. At the end of the season, they picked Joltin' Joe as the American League MVP. Here is how DiMaggio did during his 56-game streak.

Ted Williams and Joe DiMaggio

AT BATS	HITS	RUNS	HOME RUNS	RUNS BATTED IN	BATTING AVERAGE
223	91	56	15	55	.408

Fantastic Finish

DiMaggio faced Al Smith in the first inning. He smashed a ball down the third-base line. Ken Keltner gloved the ball and threw out DiMaggio. DiMaggio drew a walk in the fourth inning. In the seventh inning, Keltner made another good play on a sharp grounder. DiMaggio was 0-for-2. He would have one more chance.

DiMaggio came to bat in the eighth inning with the bases loaded. He hit a sizzling grounder to the shortstop. It took a bad hop, but Lou Boudreau speared it and started a double play. DiMaggio simply picked up his glove and ran to his position in center field. As always, he showed great poise and class.

Joe DiMaggio makes two zeroes with his fingers to show that he went hitless in his 57th game.

DID YOU KNOW?

No one has come close to matching DiMaggio's 56-game streak. In 1978, Pete Rose of the Cincinnati Reds hit in 44 straight games. No player has done better since.

#8 The Buckner Ball

The Mets Pull Off a Miracle

In 1986, the Boston Red Sox still appeared to be cursed. They had not won a championship since selling Babe Ruth to the Yankees in 1920. Boston had reached the seventh game of the World Series three times since then. Each of those games had ended in disappointment. It looked as if the Red Sox might finally lift the curse in the World Series. The New York Mets had other plans.

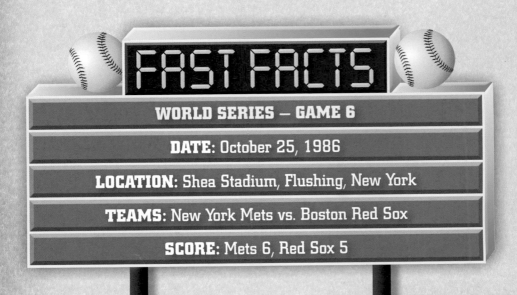

FAST FACTS

WORLD SERIES – GAME 6
DATE: October 25, 1986
LOCATION: Shea Stadium, Flushing, New York
TEAMS: New York Mets vs. Boston Red Sox
SCORE: Mets 6, Red Sox 5

Almost Over

The Red Sox had a championship within their reach. They had won the first two games of the World Series in New York. The Mets won the next two, but Boston won Game 5. The Red Sox sent their best pitcher, Roger Clemens, to the mound for Game 6. The **Cy Young Award** winner hoped to end Boston's years of misery.

Game On

Boston gave Clemens a quick 2–0 lead. The Mets fought back to tie the score in the fifth inning. Clemens was removed for a pinch hitter in the eighth. The score was knotted 3–3 after nine innings. In the 10th inning, Boston's Dave Henderson hit a long home run. The noisy fans at Shea Stadium fell silent. Many lost hope when the Red Sox scored another run. Boston led 5–3 going into the bottom of the 10th inning.

New York's Mookie Wilson sprints out of the batter's box. His speed would play a big part in the final inning of Game 6.

> **❝I don't believe in luck. I don't believe in history, either. But maybe I'm starting to.❞**
> —Red Sox outfielder Dwight Evans

FOR THE RECORD

The Red Sox won the World Series in 1918. They did not reach the Series again until 1946. That year, Boston and the St. Louis Cardinals were tied late in Game 7. Enos Slaughter of the Cardinals scored the winning run from first base on a base hit. Boston reached the World Series again in 1967 and 1975. Both times they lost in seven games. Red Sox fans had been waiting 68 years for a championship when the 1986 World Series began!

Enos Slaughter slides across the plate with the winning run in the 1946 World Series.

Bottom of the 10th

Pitcher Calvin Schiraldi was set to finish the series for Boston. A year earlier, he had pitched for the Mets. Schiraldi got the first two batters out in the 10th inning. But Gary Carter, Kevin Mitchell, and Ray Knight kept the game alive with three singles. Knight's hit made the score 5–4. Mookie Wilson came to bat. The Red Sox called on Bob Stanley to finish the game.

Gary Carter slaps a base hit. His single in the 10th inning kept New York's hopes alive.

Bill Buckner turns to look for the ball after it rolled through his legs. His error allowed the winning run to score in Game 6.

Fantastic Finish

Wilson fouled off two good pitches. He then had to jump out of the way of an inside pitch. The ball rolled behind the catcher, and Mitchell scored the tying run. On the next pitch, Wilson hit a slow grounder toward first baseman Bill Buckner. He looked up to see the speedy Wilson racing to first base. The ball rolled under Buckner's glove and through his legs. Knight scored from second base. The Mets had done the impossible, winning 6–5.

> **❝I can't remember the last time I missed a ground ball. I'll remember this one.❞**
>
> —Bill Buckner

DID YOU KNOW?

The Mets won Game 7 by a score of 8–5. Boston fans were furious. For years, they blamed Buckner for the loss. After winning the World Series in 2004, the Red Sox invited Buckner back to their stadium. The fans gave him a standing ovation.

#9 An A-MAYS-ING Catch

Willie Mays and the Giants Stun Cleveland

Could anyone beat the Cleveland Indians in 1954? Few American League teams could. Cleveland won a record 111 games during the season. Perhaps the New York Giants knew something that those teams didn't. Few things shake the confidence of a baseball team like a long out or a short home run. The Indians learned that lesson the hard way in the World Series.

FAST FACTS

WORLD SERIES — GAME 1

DATE: September 29, 1954

LOCATION: The Polo Grounds, New York City, New York

TEAMS: New York Giants vs. Cleveland Indians

SCORE: Giants 5, Indians 2

Willie Mays sends a pitch screaming into the outfield. He was the National League MVP in 1954. To beat the Indians, the Giants would need some big plays from him.

Cleveland Rocks

The Indians were one of the strongest teams ever in the World Series. The Indians pitching staff had four future Hall of Famers. Cleveland pitchers had allowed the fewest hits, walks, and runs in the American League. Indians hitters led the league in home runs. Superstar Willie Mays and the Giants didn't seem to have a chance.

Game On

Bob Lemon pitched Game 1 for the Indians. He had won 23 times during the season. In the first inning, Vic Wertz smashed a long triple to score two runs. The Giants tied the game in the third inning. The game was still tied 2–2 after seven innings.

Willie Mays raises his glove to catch Vic Wertz's long fly ball. Mays's catch shocked the Indians.

The Catch

In the eighth inning, the Indians put two runners on base. Wertz hit another long drive. Willie Mays ran to the deepest part of center field. At the last moment, he held out his glove and caught the ball as it passed over his shoulder. It was one of the greatest catches in history. Mays was 460 feet away from home plate. He spun and threw the ball to the infield. The Indians retreated to their bases. They were unable to score.

FOR THE RECORD

In the early 1950s, New York baseball fans argued about who was the best center fielder in town. Was it Mickey Mantle of the Yankees or Duke Snider of the Dodgers? In 1954, Willie Mays gave them a third player to shout about!

1954	AGE	HOME RUNS	RBI*	AVG**
DUKE SNIDER	27	40	130	.341
MICKEY MANTLE	22	27	102	.300
WILLIE MAYS	23	41	110	.345

*Runs Batted In   **Batting Average

Fantastic Finish

The game was still tied 2–2 in the bottom of the 10th inning. With one out, Mays and Hank Thompson walked. New York's Dusty Rhodes entered the game as a pinch hitter. The Giants stadium was shaped like a horseshoe. Center field was very deep, but the foul lines were very close to home plate. Rhodes **pulled** a pitch 260 feet down the right-field line. It sailed over the wall for a game-winning home run.

The Indians didn't recover from their loss in Game 1. The Giants swept all four games to become champions.

> **❝I had that one all the way. All the way.❞**
>
> —Willie Mays, on his amazing catch

Dusty Rhodes is all smiles after his home run in Game 1.

DID YOU KNOW?

The Indians faced Rhodes just seven times in the World Series—but that was enough. They only got him out twice. He homered again in Game 2. He also had a hit with the bases loaded in Game 3. Rhodes had four hits and drove in seven runs in all.

#10 The New Iron Man

Cal Ripken Jr. Passes Lou Gehrig

Baseball was in trouble in the summer of 1995. An argument between the owners and the players had shut down the season in 1994. No World Series was played. The fans were angry. Baseball needed a hero. Cal Ripken Jr. was perfect for that role. While other players showed off or complained about money, all Ripken did was the same thing regular people did. He showed up to work every day.

FAST FACTS

REGULAR SEASON BASEBALL GAME

DATE: September 6, 1995

LOCATION: Oriole Park at Camden Yards, Baltimore, Maryland

TEAMS: Baltimore Orioles vs. California Angels

SCORE: Orioles 4, Angels 2

Day In, Day Out

On May 30, 1982, Cal Ripken Jr. started a game for the Baltimore Orioles. Game after game— season after season—he never took a day off. Ripken played through the usual bumps and bruises that a shortstop suffers. He also played through painful injuries. In 1995, Ripken closed in on a record set by Lou Gehrig. The Yankees legend, known as "the Iron Horse," had played 2,130 games in a row.

Game On

Ripken tied Gehrig's record on September 5. The next night, Ripken took the field against the California Angels. The air crackled with excitement. President Bill Clinton was in the ballpark. So was Ripken's family. They jumped to their feet in the fourth inning when he blasted a home run.

Cal Ripken Jr. smacks a home run on September 5, 1995. He homered in games 2,130 and 2,131 of his streak.

> **❝All it really means is coming to the ballpark ready to play.❞**
> —Cal Ripken Jr., on what the streak meant to him

The numbers say it all as Cal Ripken Jr. takes a "victory lap" around Camden Yards.

Victory Lap

After the Angels batted in the top of the fifth inning, the game became official. Large banners hanging beyond the outfield wall changed from 2,130 to 2,131. The fans stood and cheered Ripken for more than 20 minutes. He ran around the field and gave high fives to the fans. He recognized hundreds of them. They had been coming to watch him play for 15 seasons.

FOR THE RECORD

Lou Gehrig's playing streak lasted from 1925 to 1939. During his career, Gehrig batted .340 and hit 493 home runs. He helped the New York Yankees win six World Series. The Yankees held a special day in his honor in 1939. He told the fans that he was "the luckiest man on the face of the earth." They did not know Gehrig was dying of a painful disease. He died less than two years later.

Babe Ruth gives his old teammate a hug on Lou Gehrig Day in 1939.

Fantastic Finish

The Orioles went on to beat the Angels 4–2. But the score didn't matter. No one left the stadium after the game. They stayed to hear baseball's new Iron Man. Ripken thanked the fans for supporting him for so many years. He said he was overwhelmed to be linked to the courageous Gehrig. "I'm truly humbled to have our names spoken in the same breath," he said.

❝I tried to do it the right way. I hope the fans remember that.❞
—Cal Ripken Jr., on how he played the game

Cal Ripken Jr. waves his cap to the fans in Baltimore. Many had been at the first game of his streak in 1982.

DID YOU KNOW?

Ripken would not miss a game until September 20, 1998. He played 2,632 games in a row. When Ripken retired, he held the record for most home runs by a shortstop.

Kirk Clubs the A's

World Series — Game 1
October 15, 1988
Los Angeles Dodgers 5, Oakland A's 4

Kirk Gibson of the Dodgers was the 1988 National League MVP. But he was badly injured and not expected play in the World Series. The A's led 4–3 in the bottom of the ninth inning of Game 1. Their best pitcher, Dennis Eckersley, was on the mound.

Gibson came on as a pinch hitter with two outs and a runner on base. He launched a game-winning homer to center field. Gibson pumped his fist as he limped around the bases. The Dodgers went on to win the Series four games to one.

Carter Ends It

World Series — Game 6
October 23, 1993
Toronto Blue Jays 8, Philadelphia Phillies 6

Philadelphia led Toronto 6–5 in the ninth inning. The Phillies needed three outs to force a Game 7. They called on hard-throwing reliever Mitch Williams to close out the game.

Two men were on base for Toronto with one out. Joe Carter pulled a fastball by Williams over the left-field wall. He jumped for joy as he rounded the bases. The Blue Jays were world champs. Carter joined Bill Mazeroski as the only players to end the World Series on a home run.

Glossary

bullpen: the area where pitchers warm up during games

Cy Young Award: an award given each year to the best pitcher in each league

double play: a play in which the defense gets two outs on one batted ball

farm team: another name for a minor-league team that is owned by a major-league team. The best players from farm teams get called up to the major leagues.

Gold Glove: an award given to the best fielder at each position

grand slam: a home run with the bases loaded (runners on first, second, and third bases)

Hall of Famer: one of baseball's greatest players of all time. Hall of Famers are honored at the Baseball Hall of Fame and Museum in Cooperstown, New York.

Negro Leagues: a group of leagues created for teams of African American players. Some of baseball's greatest stars played in the Negro Leagues when major-league baseball allowed only white players.

pennant: a league championship. The pennant winners of the American League and the National League meet in the World Series.

perfect game: a game in which a pitcher does not allow a runner to reach first base

pinch hitter: a player who bats in place of a teammate. When a team uses a pinch hitter, the replaced player is out of the game.

pulled: hit a pitch toward the foul line. Right-handed hitters pull pitches to left field; left-handed hitters pull pitches to right field.

rookie: a player in his first season in the major leagues

For More Information

Books

Baseball. DK Eyewitness Books. New York: DK Children, 2005.

Kadir, Nelson. *We Are the Ship: The Story of Negro League Baseball.* New York: Hyperion Books, 2008.

Stewart, Mark and Mike Kennedy. *Long Ball: The Legend and Lore of the Home Run.* Minneapolis: Millbrook Press, 2006.

Web Sites

Major League Baseball
mlb.com

National Baseball Hall of Fame and Museum
www.baseballhalloffame.org

Publisher's note to educators and parents: Our editors have carefully reviewed these web sites to ensure that they are suitable for children. Many web sites change frequently, however, and we cannot guarantee that a site's future contents will continue to meet our high standards of quality and educational value. Be advised that children should be closely supervised whenever they access the Internet.

Index

About the Author

Mark Stewart is the "ultimate" sports author. He has published more than 50 books on baseball's greatest moments, players, and teams. Mark has met many of the players in this book, including Jackie Robinson, Bobby Thomson, Willie Mays, Don Larsen, and Hank Aaron. Mark has also worked on biographies with sluggers Frank Thomas and Cecil Fielder and pitcher John Franco.